Introduction

On the tenth kilometer, a person ceases to think that he runs at all. The step acquires a certain rhythm, the breathing becomes more even, and the heart rate and heart rate are stabilized at a level that allows to maintain a certain endurance for the next long hours. After all, we become free. The tension disappears, and the rider unites with the road and the surrounding nature.

We want to run and at the same time finally see the finish line. We want this moment to last forever, and at the same time we want relief when we can finally relax in the shade of a tree or tent. When you run everything seems simple, and your problems and dreams are focused on reaching the next meter.

I have travelled many miles in my life, but not only have they prompted me to write this book. For twenty years of planning and careful writing of notes, I have experienced many successes and failures. Many times I had to stop to catch my breath. More than one time, life forced me to speed up, wanting to catch up with my plans.

I am aware that success cannot, or should not, be attributed solely to certain spheres of life. It is difficult to even clearly describe it in a coherent definition, because everything we outline will be incomplete or not entirely fitting into the current time. Success has as many faces as there are people on Earth, and it could be said that even more tens of thousands more than this, after all, a huge number.

As a long-time runner, I realize that success will always be for me both that I will stand for the race and how long I will reach the finish line. The achievement for me is family relationships, the results of my work and the fact that in good health I can start another day. There is no place in any publication for a precise description of all the emotions and feelings surrounding victory, but twenty years of reflection allows me to outline a certain framework that maintains what can be called a unique achievement on the bumpy path of our lives.

I would very much like the reader of this not very long story, contained in the form of a guide, to draw inspiration from the experiences that have worked in my case and to be able to build a solid foundation for his own dreams. Only such a foundation will allow you to create really big things, at the same time without losing all the emotions that can be experienced during this construction.

It is the road, not the goal itself, that is often the main achievement. If you read these words, it means that something has prompted you to change your life. My job is to show the direction you can go. You can – that doesn't mean you have to or should. I'm not saying that my methods are better or worse than others, but they have led me to that point in my life when I feel like sharing them. I am grateful that you have agreed to meet them.

In the book you will learn both what I think success is and how to strive for it so as not to waste time. Faith, patience, and humility, in the face of the increasing obstacles encountered on the road, seem to me necessary to feel fulfilled in any field. Great athletes and people unknown to us combine a feeling of true happiness when they feel and can actually measure their own achievements.

It all starts with dreams. This is a truth that you have already met many times, and at the same time something worth rediscovering all the time. You can't think of a change in your life without even having the slightest dream. For some it will be the construction of an office building, for others the purchase of a taxi or sending a child on a trip to a beautiful place. If our dreams are **supported by deeds,** then we can talk about the fact that we follow them even in small steps, but we are constantly moving forward.

To find out what success is, you need to get to know yourself better. Put simple tasks in front of you that will allow you to bring out a little passion and commitment every day. You may have wanted to learn how to draw, but your line remains shaky and illegible. Perhaps you wanted to fix the old car itself, which your parents or grandparents commuted to work. The best time for change is right now and it is today, at this point, that you should start working to achieve your goals.

Even the largest buildings are built, starting with a single brick. Sometimes you need to tear down the entire wall and start everything from the beginning. Both in ultramarathon and in everyday life meta and sense of fulfillment await only those who make every effort.

You can entrust your fate with a little luck, but above all you should take care to constantly help this happiness, constantly raise bricks that fall and crumble under the influence of unfavorable conditions. We all want something, but not everyone can afford to acknowledge these desires and give them more than a moment from their lives. Stop being afraid of yourself! Your dreams and goals can also become other people's dreams and goals.

The book you are reading is also intended to encourage cooperation. You can only succeed alone, but we have even more satisfaction if we can create a team that pursues the same goal.

As in other cases, start with small things. For example, you can get your family to play outdoors or learn some form of exercise to improve the mood and fitness of your loved ones.

You may find time for bigger projects, and then this book will be a useful inspiration. It is the scale that makes success even more expressive, and it is from this perspective that we will build our memories of the past. Running a marathon, you realize that you will never forget this feeling, even if you have come to live a hundred years. It's the same with your wedding, the birth of a child, or other major events in your life.

Try to initiate this type of event yourself. Forget the blind fate that leads you by the hand. Focus on creating and transforming even a small part of the world around you. Success should be created and built. Do not forget that you are the creator and builder, and it is up to you what the final shape will be your goals and life.

Opportunities, gender, social status and all other factors can be of secondary importance. We are the lords of our world, as well as our own success. Learn to look through the prism of what you want to change, not what prevents you from achieving your goals. If you remember even a few of these simple truths in the introduction, you have already become a different person from now on.

Capture your dreams and treat them as the key to something bigger and tangible. With their help, try to build what you can call success and what will accompany you wherever you take your steps.

1. You are a man of success

You may not believe the title's theme. I would like to prove to you that you really are a man of success. You probably don't have a limousine or a private jet. Your actions are probably not accompanied by media following every step.

After all, you are the most important character and it is up to you how you look at the world in the next, better part of your life. When I look at my own past, I see a lot of dark spots in it, but above all I see the power of faith and strong will that has shaped me and allows me to continue to dream of future achievements.

I've had a lot of competitions and in each of them I've tried to bring out what's perfect in me. Sometimes I've been better, other times worse, but actually every day I can find something that I can consider to be more or less successful. Today, for example, I got up in the morning to do another workout. I try to stay healthy, because it is the basis of all activities.

Without consistency and regularity, I could not even dream of entering the steep stairs of a skyscraper without shortness of breath. Before I reach the next level, I have to work many hours. This work will sooner or later turn me into two.

Your commitment is also a certain achievement of those around you. The work you do every day serves to make them better and more energetic about participating in their own activities. With this approach, nothing is a loss, and everything becomes a success.

So your first task is to look at your normal day through the prism of what you have achieved today and what you still lacked. It's not art to see great victories and moments in your life when you've become at the peak of fame. An even more important achievement is to see victories where others see only routine.

Surely, even today, you have done something that can change you for the better in the future. Only sitting idle and thinking about the enormity of one's own misfortune can be considered a complete failure. In almost all other activities you need to learn to find success.

Start with what works best for you and try to do it as much as possible. This advice is effective for the greatest champions of sport, business and all other areas where talent, skills and experience matter. It's only when you're satisfied with the task you're doing that you'll move on to other activities that you've seemed pretty abstract so far.

Nowadays, you can become who you want, and millions, fame and wealth are really at your fingertips. Success is not the lottery in which the lucky ones win. If you want to build something really big, you need to start with small bricks that are already all around you.

You are a unique person. You have an unlimited talent pool. It is from them that you will best create what you dream of. Look at your friends and people around you who are your superiors. Surely in each of them you will find something that you can envy. They have already achieved success in your eyes. It will be difficult for you to replica in this success, but perhaps thanks to such observations you will find your own way.

Speaking of victory, however, I want to firmly separate this concept from material goods. The real victory lies deep in our mind and only there can be properly interpreted and used.

The victory is the people we know and respect, the family we have built and the position at work that has often made us master what we do. If you don't feel good about what you're doing in this position, have problems at home, or generally your relationships with other people are complicated, start building your success on the most visible character traits.

You can be charismatic or patient. You may also want to show great confidence or humility. There is no single psyche model to help you get to every destination. It is your psyche that is equipped with elements that can make the most positive changes in your life.

Use who you are to become who you want to be. In life and business there is a place for both those who scream and for those who calmly take every attention. Both of these characteristics work in completely different circumstances, at the same time they can make the same progress in all areas of life.

If impatience and explosive temperament do not allow you to take advantage of the opportunities offered by fate, learn to control emotions. Sometimes retreat for a while to return much smarter and more effective. If shyness doesn't allow you to face challenges, start with small steps. Change slowly to get used to what you can achieve in the future.

Success has only one name. That's your name.

2. Don't be ashamed of your own ideas

The world is full of strange ideas and even weirder people. In fact, no idea is quite a missed idea, especially when it comes to ideas that can change your life. Remember that when you were a child, nothing seemed strange or scary enough to know and experience.

You still have the same child. You want to know and experience, even when your conscious mind says that something is incompatible with other people's expectations. Leave other people's expectations aside. After all, if you want to change, you have to start with yourself, not what others say about you.

Search and experiment all the time. Do your job, but open yourself up to other experiences as well. You can find your place everywhere. All you have to do is reach out and admit to yourself that you really are capable of achieving a goal.

"I can do it" – repeat it to yourself for hours. Practice, ask, and learn to do so. You can't want anything without admit it in front of you. For some, the dream is to become a great entrepreneur. For others – make an appointment with an attractive colleague.

If you are not sufficiently convinced of what you want to do, your goal will only be a dream increasingly sivy by the fog of reality. A good idea and its implementation – this is what every person needs. Knowing how to achieve something can come with time. When we move our own desires away from each other, then we can be sure that they will remain only in the realm of dreams.

Talk about some things out loud. Others are better kept secret until something tangible is made of them. Wherever knowledge and advice are needed, it is worth reaching out to contacts with more experienced people. If you want to create something away from other people secretly, then you are left with tutorials and tutorials on the internet. In my experience, however, sooner or later comes a time when with the idea held so far on the shelf of a dark garage you will have to go out to people.

Even the most negative ratings will not stop a man who knows what he wants. Negative feedback has always been more of an indication to me than something that would prompt me to stop. You can't change much without evaluating. Sooner or later you have to show people what you can by being prepared for every possible scenario.

The worst ideas are the unrealized ones. After all, the world is made up of successes. We are what we have succeeded in, not what we have abandoned or postponed. As children, we believe that we can achieve everything we desire. This faith goes out in us with successive failures. You have to look back boldly at your assumptions.

Finally, it is worth to publish the work on the Internet, share your own knowledge and experience, which perhaps will allow you to develop the knowledge and experience of others. Presenting an idea is another skill we lost as we grew up. I remind you that the works created by the greatest painters in their youth most often resembled shapeless spots, and yet they developed craftsmanship to such an extent that they admire millions of them.

Say to yourself, "I created this," "I invented it," and show your work to the whole world. Most likely, at first the reception will be paltry, if at all someone your plan will be interested. But isn't the child's work primarily intended for parents and friends? End with shame. You have the best opportunity to show what you can do.

Try to find a community interested in what you're doing. It may be in your city. It is also possible that you will have to seek support much further. Hiding your ideas in the closet, however, you will not find any support, and everything you create will be just your thing.

Go out and show up to the world. He is waiting for you.

3. Believe what you're doing

When you watch the struggles of your favorite athletes, until the last second you hope that they will win. Many times with family and friends you kept your fingers crossed that one plan or another would succeed a person you don't know at all. We believe in movie heroes, athletes, artists, politicians or millionaires.

We believe in a lot of things, but how poorly we can believe in ourselves. It is not easy to rely solely on self-belief. Without other activities, faith brings little, but it is often the foundation of all the achievements that will become yours. With dreams and faith, you actually have half the things you need to do even the biggest things.

Without faith in success, any plans are merely investments of time or money without emotion. It is emotions that are the main component of success. You do something to feel fulfilled, to reach a state where you will be convinced that you can do even more, and your possibilities are really endless.

Without faith, it is impossible to come to such a conviction. So why are you constantly trying to suppress a positive self-assessment? Why do you tell yourself that your ideas are just a pipe dream and you certainly won't be able to realize them. With such conviction you will stand halfway. Most likely, you will stop before you start doing anything useful.

Faith is a driving force as strong as success. You don't have to keep winning to feel like a winner. Repeated failure also does not make you a loser. If you have faith and can support it with hard work and consistency, every door will be open to you.

As you may have noticed, even in the first paragraph of this chapter, faith is very contagious. It is thanks to her that people organize themselves into groups that can achieve great things. Faith cements all relationships. In addition, it makes whatever happens, you will actually keep moving forward. Failure is just another lesson when you are convinced that the way you have chosen is the one that can bring you success.

It is difficult to believe something only on the basis of one's own conviction. True faith to succeed lies in the rationale we receive from the outside. Almost every entrepreneur went through the stage of building his small empire only on his own involvement. A large proportion of managers in charge of the world and economy base their actions primarily on how they can infect others with their faith.

Surely you have people around you who are better able to convince than others to their own views or ideas. Such leaders radiate the energy that comes from taking over the energy of others. You need a proven method to top up your belief in success, just as you recharge your mobile phone every day.

At this point, you can use textbooks or conversations with other people. One is winged by serious music and the other by heavy metal. Closing in on the opportunities offered by an inspiring world is what limits the chances of making plans very limited. Keep trying to fuel the belief that you might succeed. Search for confirmation, find as much evidence as possible of the validity of your assumptions.

This approach works in a much wider area than business. It is much easier to get rid of bad habits when it came into contact with people who succeeded. You'll learn new skills much faster to get a better job when you watch a video or listen to a podcast from someone who has gone the same way.

Faith is not a constant thing. Unfortunately, as one of the most important factors of success, he tends to completely disappear. In your plans you will probably have moments when you will lose all hope of success. It is in these moments that the fate of the changes you have decided to make will be decided.

The strongest work best when they get the worst of the floods. A total catastrophe can be a turning point if faith is strong enough to sustain dreams. It is she who creates desires and goals, not the other way around. First there is the belief that something is possible, and only later is the planning and implementation.

The more convinced we are, the more effectively our actions will change into real constructions. Perhaps faith alone will do little to solve the difficult technical problems or conflicts we have with partners at home or work. If we show that we really want to, then obstacles will become just another puzzle that needs to be solved.

If we compare success to winning a game, faith can be something that keeps the field of play and the rules on which it takes place. If you or your team no longer believe in the project, it will only become a collection of technical elements, devoid of an integral whole. Faith is therefore a kind of glue connecting elements.

Believe in your dreams so that others can believe in you!

4. Remember what you intended

How well do you remember what you wanted ten years ago? Have you achieved any of these desires? At what stage of this process are you currently in? These questions are very important for the context in which success is considered. I wanted to have a good car and that's what I'm driving right now. I wanted to learn how to play the piano, so now even the most difficult chords are not a problem for me.

I can still recall from my memory the most important elements of what I have dreamed of in the past. I realize that I still have to remind myself of the details, go back to some threads and process them again indefinitely. You need to learn from your mistakes, eliminate the most common ones. As humans, we tend to forget the bad things, but as people who want to succeed, we cannot afford it.

Our memory has a very puzzling design. He likes to get rid of what he finds unhelpful. That is why we repeatedly forget about our abilities and talents for the daily routine that brings regular money. If you look back, you will surely find things that pleased you, and in addition, you were very good at them.

In order to strengthen positive emotions and perhaps build the foundations of the original idea, it is worth reaching for very hidden corners of memory, where creativity and openness to experience are hidden. You may have played guitar a few years ago, wanting to start your own rock band. It is possible that you had an old car, which you wanted to bring to a state of usability with all your strength.

Over time, we lose our passions, but not our skills. A person who once knew French well can play it after only a few months of re-training. The same applies to every passion. So you should look for success in your memory, because that's where a lot of unique ideas are hidden.

Why did you stop running, playing double bass or making toys out of garbage? As a mature person, all these activities may seem silly, but they can make a radical change in your life. Our minds are aware of what they have been able to remember in the past, as well as what else they can learn in the future.

Limiting it to what seems safe and right is nothing more than depriving yourself of the chance to succeed.

You stopped singing, drawing or creating something of your own and unique. You have locked yourself in a world of duty, so you have confined your experience to a narrow zone from which it is difficult to get out. Try to recreate your happiest moments, moments when you were creative and thought you were able to do something even more important.

The best time to remember all this is right now, and this whole chapter is going to serve you as the engine that drives your inspiration. You already have faith in your own ideas, you can share them with others. Memory is where you have to look for the basic tools to achieve your goals.

In most cases, you don't have to create everything from scratch. As I have already written, it is worth considering creating or strengthening what is best suited. The pace of a changing world makes it difficult for us to choose something that we can actually turn into success. What was very fashionable yesterday may be quite outdated today, but there are things that seem to be universal. It is only necessary to adapt them to the present times in order to bring benefits again.

In business, for example, we tend to reproduce traditional brands and objects. The sentiment prompts people to buy music on tape and use wooden cutlery and tableware. You can find similar phenomena in your own past.

Look back and you'll find your future there!

5. Aim for success

The goal is synonymous with success for me, so you have to forgive me for giving it the longest chapter in this book. While something can be achieved by excluding one of the previous elements, it is virtually impossible to get to the point where we will be satisfied with our efforts without purpose.

You have to have a goal, just as you have to have dreams or faith. Some do not exclude the other, and Indeed I will find that they complement each other like individual instruments in a symphony orchestra. However, this objective plays a major role here. In this orchestra he is a soloist, setting the style and pace of proceedings of all other components.

Aimlessly, we move groped among the options that reality offers us. We are committed to wandering, from which it is difficult to extract something really valuable. Everything you have planned and are going to achieve must be related to a greater or lesser goal. It is he who is the highlight to reach, and it is on the basis of it that you will evaluate the quality of what you have achieved.

When setting yourself a goal, you need to have a few things in mind. First of all, it is necessary to realize what the goal is not. We will be the first to make dreams come true here. They cannot be combined with a target. From dreams only the goal arises, but in itself they are only a sketch of what is to be created in the future.

The same applies to some unidentified whims. Our personality is constantly changing. With it, what we want and what we strive for changes. At one point we want to have a sports motorcycle, and in the other we want a family van. The natural thing here is the dynamics of these changes. Our subconscious mind constantly pushes new desires.

Only a fraction of them can be identified with a target. Let's recall the analogy to the drawing. Wanting to create a work, we will bite a lot of sketches, but in fact we decide that only one of them will be the basis for the right image. Sketches that have shortcomings or are very blurry are rejected already in the initial stages. Only those in which you can see the clear contour, emotions and structure of the work remain with us.

The objective must therefore be precise, clear and precise. From this point of view, the purpose of the term "I will make a lot of money" or "I will create a popular computer program" cannot be called. These are only dreams, blurred sketches that scroll through our imagination, filling the memory.

A very important part of the puzzle that creates success is the ability to choose from them something that is most precise and well-known. Using earlier examples, the goal could be to create an app to help young people find a place where they can take an internship or learn a language within half a year until we go on a long-awaited trip to Australia. The more precisely we define our goal, the easier it will be for us to achieve it and the more motivated we will be to pursue it.

Each project should be able to accurately write down the components. Before you create a goal, you need to ask yourself and others what really creates it and how you can modify it later. Returning to the example of language learning, one can realize that this goal is the ability to read, speak and lay out texts. Moreover, in order, for example, to learn English in the Australian variety, it is necessary to know the idioms and specific terms of even the simplest things. Contrary to appearances, there are many of them and it is worth getting acquainted with them, wanting to understand australians.

As you may have already noticed, time plays an important role in shaping the goal. There is no proper purpose without a certain time. In the life of an entrepreneur and a person who cares about success, he plays the most important role. In my career, I've learned that time is not money, but much more than finance. Time motivates and establishes the routine needed everywhere. It changes us and teaches us patience, humility, and consistency. Always set goals with a specific date of achievement. The organization of time here is just as important as what you want to achieve. Getting a certain structure of habits and habits allows you to achieve almost any goal.

There are many ways to find motivation just in time. Many applications in our smartphones allow you to create a to-do list that, no less, constitutes a list of goals to achieve in a certain time. I encourage you to familiarize yourself with the different ways of organizing. Everyone has a different style of action, so it's hard to get good or bad hints here. However, I prefer to make in myself the need for punctuality and consequences very useful in almost every endeavor.

When I write this book, I add a few paragraphs every day. Some come out better, others worse, but doing so allows me to maintain a certain rhythm. Getting up in the morning has long been one of the goals I want to achieve at the start of the next day. I realize that the sooner I get up, the more things I can do and the more time I have to prepare for the tasks that await me.

. I don't plan or write it down. Getting up early is part of my personality.

When creating a goal, I need to make sure that I realistically evaluate my resources and capabilities. Overestimating your strength and resources is one of the disasters that can happen during the planned changes in your life. You should always start with small things, so that on the basis of the experience gained during their creation, you can expand and change them.

It would seem that this advice is most concerned with material matters. Her greatest strength, however, is the whole sphere of life, far from money. Change in small steps, but consistently and relentlessly. Start learning a language today so that in a few years you can use it freely in all possible forms. In this action you can find many analogies to other life situations.

It makes no sense to memorized the whole dictionary to build a single sentence. You need to learn as much as is necessary to provide information. Further education should be postponed to the next carefully planned stages. There is no unnecessary seizure or wasted time if you are consciously striving to achieve your goal.

Failures in this context are seen as lessons that allow you to choose a new option or approach a task completely differently. Many people will convince you that something you do is a waste of time. I choose a completely different approach. If what you do satiates you and brings results, then you can see that you are going in the right direction. However, the effects are often not immediately apparent. Results are another component of our goals.

There are no goals without effects, both tangible and intangible. If you think it is a success to quit smoking, then the result of this process should be, first of all, the lack of desire to reach for another cigarette. It seems very often wrong to say that we have already achieved the goal and, above all, that we do not have to try any more.

Using the teachings of sport, it can be said that hours of physical exertion serve primarily to feel better in one's own body, to have more confidence and, of course, to easily climb the stairs to the sixth or seventh floor to aunt. You will know your goals just after the results. They can surprise you in two ways. You will achieve what you have planned, or you will come out completely something else, but equally useful.

A good goal is therefore very universal. For example, if you want to build your own cryptocurrency excavator, you can also learn how computers work, the security of important data, and the importance of power consumption and energy efficiency of each kilowatt taken from an outlet. So many goals have many effects that we didn't even know existed.

It is worth while implementing these small things that we can only notice by accident. However, the target cannot be constantly changed. Its essence, after all, is a certain constancy, allowing for accurate planning. If you want to build a speedboat with your own forces, try to do so despite the setbacks. By shifting to other projects or distracting you, it will be much harder for you to build anything significant.

Set your goals and let them go. Only then will they become a reality.

6. Collect everything you need

In previous chapters, you have already learned how to build big projects with small goals and how to turn dreams into reality. What I have communicated is, of course, effective, unfortunately only to a certain extent. The success of your project will be greatly demonstrated by how you will be able to collect the materials and knowledge needed to achieve your goals.

This is such a huge subject that it is very difficult to summarise its most important elements in a few sentences. I would like you to take action right away, so I will omiss most of the economic issues related to resource theory. Resources are just going to call everything that is needed to change dreams into reality.

Before you proceed to the implementation of the plans, you should accumulate as many resources as possible that will serve you later in the venture. These resources may be of a material or intangible nature. There will probably also be people who will help and dynamise further action.

Of course, the material resources include all the fixed assets necessary to create the project. To build a building, you need to have bricks, mortar, some wood, steel and plastic. Without these things, you will not even lay the foundation, so in this case, all other aspects of the construction go to the background. Moreover, it is the same with projects that do not require so many fixed assets.

Building a popular web application, however, requires a server and infrastructure that can sustain the project online. Even the best programmer will be helpless without a computer, and your application, even the most innovative, can not do without a database or later a management center.

So it's good to start with the most expensive and important material things. First, check out what's already on the market. Secondly, set minimum and maximum costs. Perhaps your project will have to have some kind of estimate, and it is known that the funds are mostly limited.

As an entrepreneur, I have learned to treat material goods as something completely temporary. Very rarely achieve success in business those who attach themselves to one place, thing or tradition. It is the material resources that you should change most often, and it is they, contrary to appearances, that represent the least value.

Probably many of you have now opened your eyes with astonishment, but really most of the things we have can be replaced with better and more practical ones. I encourage you to do it all the time. Let's say that our goal is to create garden gazebos for people who want to relax in the open air.

The materials that will be used for this sooner or later will degrade, but the knowledge you will gain by looking for customers and meeting their sometimes very sophisticated requirements will stay with you forever. No matter what you build your gazebos from, it's important that you know how to build them, and knowledge is one of the basic intangible resources.

Intangible resources make up all that cannot be converted or converted into cash in a direct way. The basic intangible resource is the knowledge to which we will dedicate one of the chapters in this book. I would not be myself if I forgot about other very important things that are very important for building success, which should be used in every possible context.

Health and vitality are also the most visible intangible resources. You know for sure a lot of people who have built their lives and careers on these resources. Health is the most important thing to achieve and enjoy the results of success, but it alone is not enough to improve one's quality of life.

Previously, I wrote about getting rid of shyness, self-confidence, and the positive energy that consistent pursuit of different goals brings. If you've been a little energetic until now, and you've generally preferred to spend time thinking rather than acting, this book is just there to change that.

Make the most of your health and opportunities. Fight to improve your life. Lift yourself up when someone turns you over and keep going ahead, because you have the strength and energy to do so. An important part of health is youth and physical attractiveness. As you may have seen on TELEVISION, success is achieved primarily by young and attractive people.

They are the ones who show them in the media, and they are the ideal that we are all going to pursue. If fate has given you these perks, you must make the most of them. There are many industries where youth and attractiveness are valued much more than any other contribution. The first example here is the creation of a youTube channel with a large reach and even more monetization.

Monetization means you can convert your assets into real revenue, and in the case of YouTube, you can do so in many ways. Take advantage of the fact that you have a nice voice or an attractive figure. Maybe it's with these paragraphs that you'll become a local fitness star in the future, or you'll be recognized as transforming old hits into a new, original style.

As I wrote earlier, take advantage of the advantages that are already available to you, on the basis of them you can build something much larger. Communication competences are also such an obvious asset, which belongs to intangible resources. If you are well-liked and able to speak your thoughts clearly, then the path of success is open to you.

People with high communication skills are essential in any industry, especially where you constantly need to connect with old or new customers. A person who can convince others is a real treasure for the marketing department of any company.

When you're successful, keep in mind that you'll use this resource most often in the early stages of your activities. Your dreams and goals require resources that you probably don't have. Only how you can convince others can bring you closer to your goal.

Continuously learn and improve communication skills. You are sympathetic and liked by a certain group of people. For many years you thought differently. So the last resource I will describe is human capital. A group that is close to you may help you with your plans. In fact, you only need one partner to create really great projects.

Look for people who best complement what you can't. Maybe you have friends who find themselves better than you when dealing with people. You may need someone with significant technical capabilities. These people are really waiting for you to find them and achieve their goal with them.

Once again, I will remind you not to be afraid to confront your ideas with the world. Only in this way you will find someone who will support your efforts and be the perfect support at every stage of the project. Unfortunately, collaborators must be treated in the same way as material resources.

You shouldn't attach or hope to another person. All hope is in you and in your plans. Partners and colleagues should support you, but there will probably be a time when they stop doing it. Hardly any cooperation lasts forever.

Board members of large companies are changing jobs, industries and views, so even with the best professionals, it's hard to find someone really solid. Prepare for change among your colleagues. Don't feel let down when someone leaves you or fails your expectations.

 If you have dreams, goals and faith, you will surely find people who will help you realize them.

7. Get going

You have already gathered enough knowledge and resources to start changing your life. This is the moment. The better can only come in many years. It is today, and actually now, that you need to start thinking about the change that can shape your future. If you plan to get rid of the addiction, stop it just immediately.

If success is related to acquiring a skill for you, go quickly to the website to order the right course or find a teacher. However, if you want to build a thriving business, catch your phone, turn on your browser and start selling your skills and ideas.

None – well, maybe almost no goal has been achieved without action. Success may be a work of chance, but as you'll see later in the book, your main task is to help. You have just become part of my plan to change the quality of life of as many people as possible.

I was the first person to try out the advice here firsthand. I'm glad you can be the next one. Let us act and remove all obstacles. Large and small projects are built primarily on action. You may have a limited number of resources, disastrous planning, and even worse organization, but if you act with faith that you will succeed, then sooner or later it will become your stake.

Note that the biggest rich started out in the simplest industries. He was selling in a bazaar, and that one was working in a shoe store. There are plenty of opportunities around you to build something of your own and unique. Take the tools and get started. Waiting will only exacerbate doubts.

Sooner or later you will abandon your dreams and plans or, even worse, someone else will take over. In action you will find everything you have learned even from this book. It will build your confidence, indicate further goals and tell you where to get the most important resources.

If you only sit and think about what you are going to achieve, then many opportunities will be lost irretrievably. People of success are not just about thinking. They try, they get confused, and then they do the same thing again. Sometimes they repeat something hundreds or even thousands of times.

Be inspired by carpensures and other crafts. Success must be forched with hard work, chiseled from a shapeless piece of wood. The forge of your dreams is open all the time. You have to go into it and get to work. Some will have to use their physical strength, others will only have to create schemes in computer programs. No matter what you do or how you get to it.

It is important that you have the courage to start, and the rest will be easier. In every run I took part in, the hardest part was the beginnings. Many athletes experience the greatest fatigue after just a few minutes of intense exertion. You too are waiting for an intense effort. You're probably not skilled at creating what you really love.

Before you reach a state, when you do not think about what needs to be done, it will take a lot of time and nerves, but each of these moments is worth experiencing repeatedly. It is the beginning of the project that most often determines its success. Even with many outstanding specialists, the best resources and an infinite amount of inspiration, you can stumble on combining it all together.

Projects become real works only when they get through the difficult beginnings of their creation. You, too, have to wade through them. It's going to be hard, much harder than you think, but it's worth it. Time is running out.

Dedicating it only to activities that are not satisfying is a crime against yourself.

We are created to act to be active. This is how every cell of your body is built. The brain does not tolerate vacuum, which is why thoughts constantly circulate in it, constantly urging us to achieve ever greater goals. Listen to the subconscious, and you will easily force yourself to work.

I say "you will force" because success doesn't have to be a pleasure at all. What's more, every penny or hour you put into achieving a goal is a value that lacks price. Act without thinking how much it will cost you. You had time to think about collecting resources and setting goals.

Now finally move on to achieve what we call success. Don't give up when you're in doubt. The road you have chosen is full of bullets and bends. It is in these moments that your true character turns out, and it is they who determine the success or failure of the whole enterprise.

You can get stuck somewhere and lose everything, but faith and action are enough to build new goals, to move forward, thinking about something new, but never to stop. Acting, forget about unnecessary questions. Mute the noise of doubt. Just do your thing without thinking about the consequences.

The subconscious and natural instinct are sometimes the best counsellors. The longer you think about something, the less time you will spend doing something. Remember that surgeons, dentists and all other specialists in their fields do many things reflexively. The subconscious can be used on many levels.

All activities can be performed without the participation of consciousness. After all, driving a car or even using a mobile phone requires only a small commitment of thought. By acting, you just want to achieve a similar state in pursuit of your goal.

Stop being like a hamster spinning in a plastic wheel, yet still in the same place. Double-check at what stage your actions are. Sometimes you will make progress, other times you will go back a few steps. The worst thing that can happen to you is to accept the current state.

Make your efforts as far as possible to move your projects forward, and if that's not possible, sometimes it's worth going back completely to start all over again. Don't give yourself a reduced fare. Work hard just when you're stuck somewhere for good.

Find even more willpower within you. Sometimes listen to people who want to help you, and another time give a chance to a blind fate, but never stop. Achieve the smallest goals and even the most ridiculous dreams. If you have health, you also have everything you need to start a whole new life.

For people who read my book at a very mature age, I can say that based on my acquaintance with many runners, I have found that it is never too late to cover even the longest distances. Every athlete over the age of seventy will tell the basic truth:

"Success is action, failure is inaction."

8. Get the consequences

Before I started writing this chapter, I watched a stupid YouTube video, checked if my friends threw something new on Facebook, went to the kitchen to make myself a sandwich. So I lost at least half an hour. It probably took me a little bit if I forgot about the strength of the consequences.

As you can see, even those who write these words can misappropriation valuable resources only because of laziness. I have bad news for you. Most of us are really lazy beasts. We can come up with a lot of things to stop doing what we should at the moment. Before we get to something, we usually walk around in circles, trying to find at least a few reasons not to do the right thing. Most often, such reasons we manage to find.

Finding guilt in one's own weaknesses is absolutely pointless. After all, we repeat to ourselves that we will always be punctual and on the most important matters we will keep our word, at least that given to ourselves. Unfortunately, we break such errams as soon as possible.

We will always find an explanation as to why we have not withstood the decision. If you check the assumptions from the first of January half a year later, you will probably know how little, from what you intended, you have actually achieved. Laziness and lack of consistency are really very strong traits in every person.

Only those who can fight it can tell you that they have been successful. It follows that if you have made more effort than usual, you have already succeeded. Money or other material goods will only be an addition to changing your habits. That's the change I'm talking about in this chapter.

For many years I wondered why children and young people with such regularity care about important terms in their computer games. Most of them know when it will be possible to open the next inbox or get some limited item to help you reach the next level. The average teenager can easily name twenty swords, and it's hard for him to remember when he was baptized Polish.

I just want to say that our memory and attention are very selective. We are much more willing to do something that interests us and in which we make progress. It's much harder to force ourself into something where you can't see that progress. For this reason, it is young people who remember the elements of the computer game better than boring and incomprehensible objects. The same is the case with the approach to implementing the plans. Even the most difficult activities you will perform more willingly, if you see steady progress, and additionally receive a reward for it.

This is not about working on your own success. Every writer knows that the hardest thing to get through is writing the middle part of the book. Starting we always feel enthusiasm, then this enthusiasm wanes. It returns only when the end is on the horizon. Working on success, you will probably have such phases too. Your enthusiasm runs out as you act.

It is impossible to keep it at the same level as at the beginning. This chapter is designed to help you work efficiently even when you feel a lack of passion and commitment. Consistency is the best way to fight laziness. The body quickly gets used to routine activities. But you have to help him.

Some are the most productive when the boss yells at them all the time, and noisy roadworks are underway outside the window. Others work best when they do a small part of a larger task every day. Only 20% of your efforts will affect 80% of the effects. This economic principle works in every area of life. Consistency will help to effectively work out these 20%. Without it, all our efforts will largely be a waste of time.

How to force ourself to act? The world's coldest people have already thought about this problem, but unfortunately each of them sees the solution very differently. In my opinion, it is the moments when you have the least desire to act that are the most effective. It's not art to work out something positive under the influence of passion and an avalanche of positive emotions. The trick is to do something practical when you really don't want to do anything.

I do not urge you to regularly devote time from 8.00 to 15.00 to implement your own plans. This model was considered inefficient long ago. The analyst works most of the day watching movies on Netflix or talking to colleagues about something completely irrelevant. Only a small part of his working time is a work that brings results.

The time comes to solve or lay out a difficult equation, and that's when the analyst has to focus all his attention. In such competitions you are like a goalkeeper of a good football team. Very often he stands there just to catch the ball once in 90 minutes. After all, he remains the most important person in the team.

Set your own rhythm of the day and work according to it. Any guides you read can give you tips, but it's up to you to establish an individual work plan. No one will do it better than you. The work plan will certainly be useful, so I strongly encourage you to draw it up, but among the greatest geniuses of many there were also those who in their surroundings and mind had a total mess. However, this did not prevent them from achieving really great successes.

While you can draw inspiration from a sport where success depends on every minute of active life being carefully planned and executed, you don't have to. Consistency is more than planning. You only make progress if you are constantly moving forward. Sometimes the time distance between one step and the other can be very large, but if you take this step, you will already succeed.

There are writers, athletes or businessmen who have been creating one project all their lives. For example, the rolex creator has only been involved in modernizing and reducing watches since his early teens. It is to him that we owe the shape and functionality of smartwatches. He didn't even dream of so many features in such a small device.

Be consistent at your own pace, and in the end you will create the project you dreamed of.

9. Money, money and money again

You need money to succeed. That's what common sense says, but it's not entirely necessary to listen to it. As I have convinced you – I hope – in previous chapters, you can successfully call everything you buy for money, but not yourself. You can have whole mountains of money, but if you don't invest it, it will only be a number in your account without any meaning.

To understand the relationship between success and money well, you need to look at the chart of any cryptocurrency. I remind you that cryptocurrency differs from any other money in that it is not guaranteed by any central bank. From this point of view, it has less value than the Ladybug card, because the Ladybug card is always paid for by this well-known store, and at some point each cryptocurrency will meet a fate such that it will become quite worthless.

I like to invest in the latest technologies, which is why I look closely at the cryptocurrency market. Having one Bitcoin, the moment I write these words, will make you a pretty rich man. One Bitcoin has the value of a good class car, and probably its price will increase even further in the near future. But even having thirty Bitcoins in your cryptocurrency wallet -you will not be rich.

The money that lies in the account just rots there. They are completely worthless. The value gives them things you can buy for them. Unfortunately, inflation and other economic developments are causing a huge change in the value of money. A hundred dollars at a time of cowboys' clashes with the Indians was a really big deal. A thousand dollars is almost a fortune for which you could buy a herd of cows. Today, for the same hundred dollars, we will buy only the tail. That's how the value of money has changed over time.

I am of such an age that I remember what it was like to be a millionaire, because by the denomination of gold everyone was him. That's when I started thinking seriously about business, because I knew that youth and every penny, or actually every hundred thousand zlotys, could bring me closer to fulfilling my dreams. I encourage you to invest your funds, even if they are very limited.

With a little skill, you can replace the pencil with a Mercedes. We need to constantly search for opportunities for money to accompany us at work. They are really workers who have to do the same as we do ourselves. If you have a hundred zlotys, you can buy a hammer, a trowel and a few adhesives for it. This is how the construction company was created, dealing with the finishing of bathrooms.

What about the fact that you probably have no idea how to lay glaze and terracotta? If you're still afraid to try it, you won't know if this work will bring you closer to bigger dreams. Saving is good for your grandfather and grandmother or dad and mom. You have energy and you should turn it into the results of your work.

Everyone would like to invest in stocks and cryptocurrencies in order to finally make a huge fortune. However, it may be better to start by investing in a regular hammer, bus or some other item that can make a profit. Investing in securities does not exclude building something with your own hands.

The more things you do with your own money at the same time, the more chances you will have to multiply them. I've written before to teach you to focus on smaller or larger goals. I still maintain this position, but I remind you that you can do one thing and your money something completely different.

While you're laying tiles, the shares you buy can gain value. A plot or property is a very good starting point for a novice investor. No matter what economic situation is on the market, real estate is the ones that attract the most attention in long-term investments. They can be rented, sold or exchanged, but it is very unlikely that they will lose value just like the money itself.

So we've already established that the component of success is everything you can buy with money, but it gives you much more opportunities. Having money opens up whole new horizons and as a person striving to know the different faces of success, you can now understand them If your passion is motorcycles, you can start an organization dedicated to them. The social value of money is not to be underestimated, so consider how much of your funds you will spend only for yourself, and how much to develop your own environment.

Success and money – this is largely the way we change the immediate environment. No one will remember if you had three cars or maybe twenty, but many people will remember the Aquapark sponsored by your company. At some stage, the way you can integrate into your environment will be the main carrier of success.

Stop tinging banknotes under your pillow and constantly enumerate tables in a spreadsheet.

Get your money to work. Learn how to manage them under different conditions. Note that if you hire someone to do things like make a website, it's money – not the contractor – that's the main culprit in your idea. If you have money, it's much easier to realize everything you come up with.

Problems start where there are long-term account gaps. When talking to someone about their own plans or successes, it should be remembered that sooner or later the question of money will be raised. Everyone would like to build great palaces, but unfortunately there is a lack of resources for this. Therefore, always talk about your capital realistically. Instead of building a pool, you might want to start with a pond first.

The contractor counts on your money more than on passions and good intentions. You can use your communication skills to convince someone, but fast transfer is a much more effective motivating measure here. Prepare your budget on this basis. It is worth dreaming about big things, but it is much more practical to think about what you have the resources for, and only in the future to expand your goals and create more complex plans.

Make plans with the help of money, because it is much easier. There are, of course, cases of creating something without money, but a well-thought-out budget will much better convince any investor to your idea than even the best visualizations. When looking for a partner or sponsor, always include the phrase: "In a few months or years, the investment costs will pay back."

When it comes to personal goals, such as quitting smoking or acquiring piano skills, costs are of secondary importance. One man will be able to play all of Mozart's works after a few weeks of study, and someone else will need long years to do so. If you finally hear beautiful music in your room or living room, played by you, then you will know the true taste of success.

As a side note, the aforementioned Mozart composed quite simple works. The real challenge is learning chopin's game. That is why Chopin competitions are organized all over the world, not Mozart competitions.

From a success point of view, money is secondary. Their value can be easily described by the amount of memories that can be purchased for them. If you buy the best bike for what you earn, then you will remember this event for a very long time. You can have a lot of bikes, but one of them will probably turn out to be a special one.

You can get it as a gift from the person you love or admire. You can also purchase it for your own money. Positive memories in both cases will be very similar.

When thinking about success, it is worth forgetting about money for a while. Probably many of you dream of starting a thriving company. For this task, initial capital is of course necessary, but much more capital is: knowledge, experience and passion that we can put into our project.

It is the tandem of passion with capital that builds a strong sense of satisfaction and, consequently, success. One without the other loses a lot. With money, but without passion, you will probably spend it on things completely irrelevant. Passion alone is not enough, because it is money that allows us to carry out plans, and it is often the size of our goals that depends on their quantity.

Anyone with a salary set at a high level for a longer period of time will at testify that at some point they stop thinking about money, and begin to change with their help for the better. Hence all the charitable activities and the desire to support the other person. It is the social role of money that is so important for understanding people's success.

A high-level payout allows you to join the group of people who have long ago ceased to worry about how to make ends meet. Together they spend time, suggest to each other, and eventually follow these actions more opportunities to multiply their capital. It is worth getting to know someone rich not to invest in us, but perhaps to convey his knowledge and at least briefly introduced to the world of business.

10. Forgive yourself and others

In recent years, the world of big business has returned to its roots. The pervasive fashion for slim management is changing the way we view corporations, public benefit organizations, and even our own finances. Everywhere they tell us that less is more, and in ascetic we will find true happiness.

I will turn back a little bit to this way of thinking, because, as the history of Buddha shows us, or at least a few well-known millionaires, neither in poverty nor in the richness of happiness, there is really no happiness. The basis of this state is living according to ourselves and doing something that makes us constantly move towards a better version of ourselves.

In achieving this, financial resources and motivation will be useful, but it is the conversation with our own subconscious that often determines how willing we are to face the problems we encounter along the way. How many times have you admitted what you really want? How many times have you tried to explain your desires and goals to yourself? Such a dialogue can be extremely helpful at every stage of our activities.

No matter how far we are from achieving our goals, it's worth constantly explaining to ourselves why we want to achieve something that seems beyond our reach. In this conversation, the topic of failure, discouragement and lack of motivation often arises. Then we have to learn to forget what was there and look only in front of us.

After all, you only live in the future. The past, though important, is merely a baggage of experience, which can sometimes weigh on very much. Invented in far away Hawaii, the ho'oponopono method is one of many ways to engage in dialogue with your inner self. For a moment or a long time, it allows you to look at yourself and your problems from someone else's perspective.

For this reason, with its help, we can realistically assess our failures and achievements. The creators and practitioners of this form of meditation suggest repeating the following mantra: "Sorry, thank you, forgive me please, I love you." In order to clear your mind, you need to apologize to yourself and others for your conduct and shortcomings. It's good to do this in a group of family or colleagues.

Our personal mantra begins with saying "I'm sorry" – for example, "I'm sorry I mis-invested the company's money, I apologize for not trying to get enough money to achieve the goal." Later, we should thank everyone for what they have done for us or simply for the fact that they exist in our lives. You can say, for example, "Thank you for agreeing to accompany me in these difficult times."

The next step is to ask for forgiveness, for example: "Forgive me for my mistake. I ask you to show me a little patience." The last most difficult, but both the most important step, is the confession of love. Let's not be afraid to say, "I love you," even when it comes to co-workers. This statement is about expressing respect and admiration for the achievements of the other person rather than the love elation described in romances.

Interestingly, it has been repeatedly proven that these exercises have a very positive effect, above all in internal dialogue. You have to love yourself to understand others. In order to do this, you must first forgive yourself, apologize for your mistakes and give yourself the opportunity to correct them. If we sincerely do not love ourselves, then our success will be incomplete, and its imperfection will give us more problems than benefits.

The best athletes forget their mistakes, because they know that in a moment or even after a long time they will have a new opportunity and opportunity to present their talent. Every stumble weighs on our conscience. Living with a ballast of failures, it's hard to take steps forward. Our problems in the past and lack of admiration for ourselves are like a big backpack with stones, which too often lures us to the chair or couch in front of the TV.

It's time to finally get rid of it. Get to know yourself better, forgive yourself for mistakes and love who you are and who you want to become. Change is the goal of success. If the only thing in this book is that you start to better understand your behavior and expectations, then you have already been very successful. From now on, when you talk to someone about what you want, start with the above formula of events, and perhaps you will become more honest, concrete and believable.

This method in itself is not part of negotiation or any other business communication, but is the starting point for this type of communication at all. Disagreement with oneself often results in a lack of understanding with other people, and this is an easy way to deny any success.

Live and follow what you think is valuable, but don't be afraid to talk about it, even in your thoughts.

11. Create your own style

In cognitive psychology classes, each student gets the following exercise. It is necessary to describe as accurately as possible what is seen in the picture. The picture is the same for all students, but its description every time seems different. Even a simple geometric figure can be described in many ways. One of us looking at the triangle will see the pyramid, the other will see a warning sign.

Both answers are correct. When interpreting an thing or event, an incorrect answer cannot be given. It would seem that the triangle will always be a triangle and nothing else, but it is a view that can block any progress in our lives. Your experience, knowledge and imagination constantly build new and unique things. Allow yourself to look at the world in an individual way. The aforementioned triangle can become an innovative building if you want it and, most importantly, you will strive for it.

Over the years of schooling, we have learned that there is only one good solution. We have been treating our whole lives as a test where we have to get the highest rating. School kills individualism in us so much that we are constantly looking for the right answers. In order to achieve success, you need to do it in your own individual way, and also at your individual pace.

Harrison Ford got his first major role in the film at the age of 35. At the time, he was a carpenter and worked as a teacher on a film set. It wasn't until after he made the Star Wars series that he became a recognizable star. You can probably see the silhouette of Indiana Jones or Han Solo in front of your eyes at this point. Great characters have their own individual style, which is hard to make a er one.

Such an image, of course, consists of physical appearance, the way of communication and visible habits and habits. Everyone knows at least a few people who can be characterized by a single trait. There are parents everywhere who speak too loudly and aunts who can talk about distant relatives all day long. Such small nuances are about a person's style. In business, however, this needs to be extended to a few other characteristics that make it easier for some to succeed only by who they are and how they behave in the face of big money.

Elon Musk is recognizable for his charisma and intransigence. If someone can fly to Mars or find an alien civilization on a distant planet, it will probably be this American visionary. He doesn't have to speak up or somehow present his own ideas. It is enough for it to appear, and already it can impose its will on others.

If you are looking for the most expressive description of style, you should look into the mid-seventies of the twentieth century. It was then that the media was ruled by one man, a young actor from Hong Kong, who made a gigantic career in Hollywood, even though he played only one film. Bruce Lee, however, was primarily an entrepreneur who, from an unpopu popular field such as martial arts at the time, made a thriving business.

He appeared in films, but he was not the best actor. He cannot be denied business skills based on promoting one's own person and image. "Be like the water that breaks the stone," he said to his fans. In doing so, he affirmed that it was necessary to be able to adapt to the existing situation, not to fight at all costs against adversity, which we will not be able to change anyway.

It's a very wise advice in life and business, but we can learn more from the star by observing the way he spoke and how he was able to match people. Like many other famous people, he paid great attention to the quality of the thoughts he pronounced. Everything he said seemed to flow out of his natural inspiration. Watching interviews, you do not see an ordinary person, but someone moreover – almost an alien.

So far, no one has managed to fake his style. Recall that this is a man who, unlike other actors and businessmen, has not achieved such great success. However, it was unique, which so far inspires generations of people who want to inspire others.

Let's break down bruce lee's advantages into individual elements. He was certainly a very handsome and energetic man. He was certainly an icon of Asian culture in America and Western Europe. He was able to speak beautifully, and most importantly, what he said actually reached the audience. He was also considered an extremely kind and sympathetic person, which in every area of life is brought by many friends and colleagues.

All this made him able to sell what he had the best and in addition build on it a solid foundation for his business and acting career. Recall that we are talking about a man who came from a moderately wealthy family. He was An American, but he belonged to the Chinese minority, which made him vulnerable to racism. After all, it is his character and silhouette that is easier to remember than thousands of CEOs and hundreds of other millionaires from Polish and around the world.

It's time to break free from the beaten patterns, forget about how people judge you. Finding your own style also allows you to create a group of people who share your vision and views, support you in your common pursuit of your goal, which, as I wrote earlier, is important for achieving it.

As I point out in this chapter, your person's strengths or flaws are completely irrelevant here. It is from these apparent flaws that you can create an explosive mixture, allowing you to stand out from others fighting for the same prey. If you can use even an apparent obstacle for your purposes, you will be able to transform the whole world around you.

No matter what gender you are, what education or abilities you have. It's important that you turn what you have into real working tools. Why is the ability to solve problems so little? If someone can win a complicated puzzle game, probably not much of it moves on to the rest of their career. It is also the case with physical condition and abilities that go beyond accepted norms.

If you have a passion for sport, just add a little effort and patience to build a certain group of people around you who want to use your skills. Even the most complex content will find its audience. People can make business out of literally everything.

Enthusiasts of old Mikrus cars can swap their garage hobbies for something much bigger and benefiting other people. When building your own image, it is worth focusing on internet technologies. Today, we are not judged solely by how we perform in interviews or television. We ourselves need to make sure that we build an interesting profile of publications that others watch about us on the internet.

Bruce Lee's method is still valid, but nowadays it would have to expand into cyberspace as well. So your style must be visible in two planes. First, try to consistently cultivate the qualities that make you stand out so that you can be known in just one word or after you look. Secondly, you need to find a way to bring these perks online.

Be like Bruce Lee.

12. Technology

Speaking of success, you can not forget about communication technology. When I write this, the most important area of business is the internet. Probably in a few years we will move to completely new areas, such as virtual reality, artificial intelligence or neuromarketing. Perhaps in the world of the future, the owner of a thriving company will be able to upload software straight into the human brain, just as he uploads it to his mobile.

Even with the simplest mobile phone, we don't realize that it really works all the time for smaller and larger corporations. Every free game or application, designed to facilitate our task, has a second bottom, thanks to which the owner of the software knows exactly what we do and what we need.

A terrifying vision of reality, where everyone knows everything, becomes very real. It is thanks to AI-based technology that shops are aware of the

, what offer to offer you, and the search engine can predict what you will need in the near future.

Your everyday life is becoming more automated, and many classes have long since lost their importance. Translators, lawyers or even marketing professionals now have a difficult transition period, as a large part of their classes have taken over the written program. Thinking about success, think about automation at the same time.

Let's start with how much technology can help you achieve your goals. Since it exists in every area of life, surely your success will depend more or less on it. Today we stop thinking what we can do or achieve ourselves, but we should also be aware of what the machine can do for us.

If you want to make money for your dream investment, there are plenty of ways where only technology can take care of you in your work. Perhaps the most obvious of these is a cryptocurrency excavator. For those who do not know anything about this thriving industry, I will say that digging cryptocurrencies is a very good way to legally raise capital at a very small cost.

A group of people agreed quite recently that the money produced by the computer has real value, in addition, they have created a technology that makes this money impossible to counterfeit. By purchasing a properly configured computer, you can create this money yourself. Bitcoins, Ethereum, Tether, Ripple are the most popular cryptocurrencies at the moment, but the situation can change dramatically when the market decides that one of them is worthless.

By building a device that will create a certain cryptocurrency for you, you will have living cash without any contribution of work. The only cost of production here is the price of one kilowatt of electricity collected. When cryptocurrencies are expensive, the investment pays off, when they lose value, it becomes unprofitable at all.

Modern technical solutions, however, help not only in raising money. With their help, you can achieve much bigger and more important goals. Algorithms that solve social problems are worth as much money as real businesses. Few know that Bill Gates' first occupation was to create an app that changed traffic lights at intersections to eliminate traffic jams.

The solution was very innovative, but it didn't work well, which is why Bill Gates is known as the creator of the Windows operating system, not as the one who solved the problem of traffic jams during rush hour.

The two examples given above are very clear and difficult manifestations of the impact of technology on success. Even without aspirations to build complex technical solutions, it is worth incorporating technologies into your plans. However successful you are, start with a decent website. If possible, go to task automation. Use computers and robotics to help you reach your goal.

You don't have to be Bill Gates or a financial genius, but you can already purchase a remotely operated excavator or drone that can photograph the large area where you are planning your investment. The more efficiently you use technology, the bigger and more accessible your goals will become. Technology works easily together, so combining even a remote-controlled excavator, drone and website can create future-facing construction and repair services.

Be very human, but make a robot work for you.

13. The art of innovation

Today I picked up a package from a parcel. It's kind of an ordinary job that everyone has done many times, but looking at it from a businessman's perspective, we can see how successful it is that I can approach a machine that will give me my shipment. There are many parcels near my house. At any time I can choose where the package can be placed, so that I can pick it up in the most convenient place for myself

You'll probably think that this whole event is related to technology, because, as I wrote in the previous chapter, you have to use the advances of technology in almost every field. The example of parcels is more than just a tool for distributing shipments. It is an excellent model for how to combine technology, logistics and an extraordinary idea for using a market niche

So I consider innovation not only an application, a website or a robot that can make its own coke. Innovative is an idea that changes your or others' lives. The first innovation, of course, was to plant grain instead of chasing the game. It happened about ten thousand years ago, and since then people are constantly coming up with something new. You too can, and should, create something extraordinary on your own.

As I have shown, innovation in one's own behaviour or in certain social relationships is the most enduring. There are still new ways of doing business or managing finance. Numerous theories are also emerging about communication, encryption and data transfer and the participation of individual social groups in a market economy.

Each of us is innovative because we all have different ways to deal with problems. Even within the same profession or group of machines, there is a variety of applications. Let's consider, for example, how you ride a bike.. Most people just get on it, using it like a regular means of transport or a fitness device.

Simply type the phrase "cycling" into the video search engine to see how many new patents are constantly being created in this area. Looking for a bike for a young family member, I found out how much progress has been made even on non-electric bikes.

Let us consider, for example, the illuminated wheels. Thanks to this, the bike is visible on the road from afar after dark. The leading cyclist can feel safer, and besides, it attracts the attention of passers-by and stands out from the crowd of bikes without this additional feature. If you're thinking about success, it's a good idea to consider what you're doing a little differently than others. Surely you are doing something that does not cause you difficulties, and in others arouses jealousy.

My neighbor has been able to grow cabbage for a long time. When there is practically not a single head on the surrounding plots, she collects them in dozens and is surprised that nowhere else has she grown up. Such a skill as planting cabbage seems insignificant, but in the right hands it can become the foundation of a thriving business. We can talk about an innovative method of sowing and breeding this common vegetable.

It allows you to think about mass popularization. With little financial investment, for example, this ability can be used to set up a company focused on selling cabbage. Thanks to efficient harvesting and a well-planned supply chain, it will bring great profits and even greater satisfaction.

Those who do not use their innovation potential are, of course, teachers and students. Only a handful of them can implement methods that work not only under certain conditions, but also in a larger population. Every parent today knows what an electronic journal is, the Classroom learning platform, and the Microsoft Teams audio and video conferencing program. These tools have helped in difficult times of isolation, but educational opportunities do not end there.

Each student introduces their own methods to accelerate and improve the quality of their learning. These include ways to use mobile phones to get information from two sources at the same time. If you're a student or student, take a look at how you're learning, and perhaps this will create a gateway to opening a new career. You're probably using something that helps you pass exams or get good grades. Perhaps making these methods public will make you earn money from them and constantly improve them.

It is only for a hundred years that we have witnessed dynamic solutions in the field of social innovation. If we take business management as an example, it is very different from what was practiced in our fathers and grandparents' day. New patterns are constantly coming in, and the role of individual positions in our company is constantly changing. It used to be a high specialization, so the employee who took his place at the production line probably stayed with her until retirement. Now we focus on more frequent changes, because they motivate progress.

You can occupy multiple positions in one company, and sometimes even several of them at once. Innovations that improve work efficiency are local and global. Workplace change is the global nature of social innovation, but there may also be ways in your company to motivate employees or make better use of their talents and passions.

Art plays an increasingly important role in many office tasks. The Japanese sing with their colleagues every week. No one asks them if they know how to sing a nice voice. Joint activities increase efficiency and innovation, and this is what you should first of all pay attention to when building an organization.

I will risk saying that there is no success without innovation. It is practically impossible to reinvent something, but innovation is also about improving the methods used for years. But to think about improving something, you need to know and understand it – and for that you need knowledge.

We should start by disasssing an activity or device into smaller pieces. It is the improvement of these small elements that allows you to create a whole new process. Let's go back to the pack where we were at the beginning of the chapter. The idea with parcels is really ordinary postal and courier services, but more automated.

One box storing packages served as a milestone for originators to create a thriving business. Thanks to it, postal services eliminated the need to queue and wait for the shipment. No one likes to wait, so every minute is valuable for both the customer and the trader.

Linking innovation over time becomes the main objective of many companies. It is now that it is important to shorten every process as much as possible, making the most of every opportunity. If you can do something faster than others, no matter what it is, you will succeed.

Faster usually means less accurately, but as the example of a parcelomat shows, accuracy is not always the highest value. We prefer to pick up a package from a machine than go to the post office, stand in line and sign receipts. Important mail shipments are still safer, but those with less value can be shipped more modern methods.

Now let's see what's innovative for the purposes you've created. I warn that only those ideas that introduce something new will bring material benefits. I will also remind you that in my book, material benefits are always at the forefront of the changes you can make in your life through your pursuit of success. Even when your efforts are not about material issues, innovation is a key to opening up a whole new way of looking at the world.

Take, for example, the problem of weight loss. At every step, you are offered a certain diet, bringing such or other benefits to your health or figure. Following only one way does not seem to be optimal, because as we have already mentioned, each of us is an individual. If you want to lose weight, it's worth trying two ways, modifying them a bit, and introducing your own.

Make sure your success is an innovation.

14. Look at the neighbor

All too often, success books give examples of visionaries like Bill Gates, Elon Musk, and other characters seen on TV all the time. We know their biographies and the most creative advice. We can identify their families, friends and even the cars they drive. Maybe you'll tell me, what success did Prince Harry achieve? His greatest achievement is that he is known or that he is a prince. His advice cannot be effective for Mrs

Sophia, who is a plumber. Prince Harry, however respected and popular, can bring little to your life.

Reading about his habits is nothing like what you can use in your life. After all, you probably won't be given to take the Duke of Monaco or go on safari with the UK Finance Minister.

It is very good to draw inspiration from people who have achieved so much in their lives that they are famous or rich. However, we should pay much more attention to our own surroundings. Most successful people are anonymous. People with huge capital or managing large companies very often shop at the Supermarket,own ten-year-old cars or take care of the garden with their own hand. Every day you are not able to recognize who of us is a man of success and who is still working on it.

In the past, the situation was simple. In the Middle Ages, one look was enough to distinguish a poor man from a rich man. We are visual scientists, so we are looking for signs of wealth in appearance so far, but unfortunately we have not found a clear confirmation there for several decades. I know a lot of influential people, and I really have to tell you that even after many years of contact, they rarely know that they have such power, money and experience. Each of them took a completely different path, but they all found their own ways to succeed.

For many years of running a business, I have found it worth getting to know the biographies of famous people, but it is even more worth looking at your own surroundings. From today, I would like your idol not to be a character from a movie, a book and a television, but a neighbor from another settlement, or the same city. We are fascinated by sending a rocket towards Mars, but we cannot appreciate the modern factory that was built near where we live.

We look at the behavior of millionaires, being indifferent to the fact that our neighbor in a few years has made a new Volvo. It is in the immediate vicinity that we should look for inspiration, because it is here, not on Mars or in New York, that we will look for opportunities to fulfill our dreams. People from our village are often more innovative than those we read about on internet portals. It is much easier to create great things, having millions of dollars in your account. It's harder to make those millions with almost zero.

Many careers and success stories are built on what's at hand. The creator of rolex was not a watchmaker, but he practiced with a watchmaker. He reduced the movement and dial of the watches so that it fits on his hand. Since then, popular pocket watches in those days have lost their importance. It was first thought that such devices were less accurate than traditional designs, but Wilsdorf insisted on his concept until he convinced others to do so.

He didn't invent watches from the beginning. Working with a watchmaker for many years, he saw how it is possible to improve existing devices and on the basis of this experience created the most famous watch business in the world. He didn't look for an idea in books or movies. He took advantage of his own work and the resources he had. He helped the most famous craftsmen in his trade, so he already had the advice and parts needed to build his idea. Even without leaving the studio, he could constantly test more prototypes, until he finally managed to create this dream.

Since ancient times, master-student relations have been the basis of all inventions. Now this has changed a lot, but still this most traditional method of acquiring knowledge and inspiration has a huge impact on most careers. Take a look at how people in your city are executing their plans. Find successful people in your field. You may already be employed in a company where the process or product can be modified.

Don't be afraid to ask and be rejected. Even a negative response to your plans is a kind of step towards their implementation. If your neighbor has somehow managed to earn a new Volvo, you too may have a similar plan. If a friend lost fifteen kilograms before her cousin's wedding, you too can achieve this by searching for your own ways to lose weight.

There are plenty of heroes around you who have been successful one way or another. Everyone is a hero, because we are all extremely talented in some field. From a German teacher, you can borrow the way he infects other people's moods. A lady from a veggie will tell you how to get rid of stubborn stains on white t-shirts, and your mechanic will tell you how to add oil to the engine you have in your car.

Success often does not consist of great things, but small hints that can fold into one coherent picture. From today, try to bring out the best of your skills, surroundings and the people you come into contact with every day. A good example here is language learning. A very ineffectual method is during it the use of only exercises and instructional videos. It is much more effective to meet the other person and learn with them, even online.

I say here with all the knowledge that my definition of success is first and foremost what you can achieve with the work, talent and resources you surely have. We don't have to build big projects right away, but it's definitely good to use what's around us. You can't afford to waste resources. Even on a few hectares of the field, you can grow an innovative variety of strawberries, even more drought-to-drought.

Without a field, strawberries can also be grown. Just get to know the farmer who will enter the company with us. Looking for local opportunities and opportunities is the basis of every country's action. What would your city be like if a few or dozens of people didn't have the courage to invest in it? Every shop or service establishment you pass on your way to work or school is a real picture of the success you can have in participating.

15. Now knowledge

Rhythm, harmony and melody are the three elements that make up each piece of music. These are also three elements that all people who want to learn how to play a piano or other instrument practice. Without any of these components, the music will sound like a mere squeak, so if you want to learn how to play

Beethoven or Allan Wake, you have to master them all to at least a basic degree.

The same is true of success. To achieve it, you need to master a lot of skills to at least a basic degree. Already in this book I have outlined a few of them to you, but the list is by no means finished. In pursuit of success, it is important both the knowledge you already have and the knowledge you can gain in the near future.

Learning is part of success, because learning is a success in itself. If you learn complex chords and musical terms, you'll be richer at understanding the melodies you listen to on internet radios. If you understand the basics of economics and management, you will know what to do so that your company does not see the spectre of bankruptcy. Both of these areas can be combined into a cool business and career idea, as there is still a lack of musicians and, above all, people who can teach this music efficiently.

It is your responsibility to learn. You never know enough that you can't discover something new and interesting. As I said recently, "success always strives for innovation", and innovation is all about knowledge. Whatever you do, you should become better, look for new solutions, and constantly change existing ones. Even if your goal is to cook the perfect beet soup, you shouldn't stop at what you already know and can do.

Man is equipped with a natural need to get to know. The older we are, the more we convince ourselves that science for beginners is primarily for children and young people, and as adults we need to focus our attention on what is practical. This approach is, of course, sensible and in most cases justified by many examples.

I wrote myself so that first of all you try to achieve greater success in what you do best, but this does not relieve you of the obligation to acquire knowledge where you have not yet reached. Perhaps the solution to your problems lies in learning programming. This is the best example of how you can combine abilities from many fields and develop brand new ones. Even the most basic programming lessons will give you a fresh view of solving all kinds of problems. By learning how to write code, you will learn the correct organization and relationship between different unrelated structures. Developers adopt new technology better and faster, because for them every thing is new.

When looking for knowledge, start with the basic elements that the school completely ignores. Learn to speak nicely, readily write with calligraphy, and perhaps even dance some exotic dance. All these skills are needed in business as much as learning English, but we can't always use it.

In 19th-century England, students from the upper ecbes were able to speak well, run after a rugby ball and keep diaries in different languages. Mathematics and science came to the fore, and britain became the greatest empire of all time. It will be difficult for you to become a brain surgeon, but nothing prevents you from learning a modern approach to recruiting and acquiring talent.

Today, economics is the basis for thinking about success. You don't have to learn complicated patterns and definitions here. Excellent economists were our grandmothers, who were able to give ten grandchildren one chocolate bar, and each of them was satisfied. All the skills you have depend on your economy. You decide how you manage them.

I hope you have found a lot of knowledge and inspiration in this book. First of all, I expect you to reach out to other publications to learn more about the topics you are interested in. It would be good if you read things that you are not interested in at all, because among them there may be a way to your personal success.

The more you know, the more chance you will have to choose the best for you. Manuals, pages and courses on the internet do not see your shortcomings. Whether you're young or old, capable, or incapathable in a field, all you need to do is take the time to learn everything you want to know.

Only science will push you forward in a controlled way. You can succeed by accident, but the satisfaction will be much greater if you know what you are doing. Even if you have not necessarily consciously succeeded, try to find out why it worked out, and you may be able to repeat your success.

Referring again to the culinary context, I can say that the success is not to make good jam from cherries and pears. Success will only come when we fix the recipe on this jam and be able to do it in any circumstances. Thanks to knowledge, success is repetitive, and what we have managed before, we are able to improve even more.

Returning to delicious jam – making the most accurate recipe for it allows you to get to completely different aspects of preparing desserts. You may discover in your recipe to limit the number of calories or the amount of sugar. Perhaps you will become the owner of the idea for the technology of storing your product without unnecessary chemicals. The number of possibilities associated with a simple jar of jam is practically unlimited and it is up to your will whether you want to improve your knowledge about it.

As you have seen in the chapter on drawing information from your neighbors, I do not require formal education here. Many of the most well-known entrepreneurs have not completed higher education or graduated in a completely different field from the one that accounts for their income. After all, someone has to deal with areas such as childcare, and they don't teach it at school.

Examples of business not related to formal education are without a few. Is there a school for youtubers? Is it possible to become a master's degree in computer games? Not too much, and for many people it is a basic livelihood.

The knowledge you acquire should be practical, as in the jam production example. You learn to benefit you in one form or another. The more you know, the more opportunities you will have to use, but try most to find out what you need.

As an entrepreneur, I recommend delving into the issue of communication, because no matter what you plan, it is important that you are able to convince others to do so. Try to find out something important in your trade every day. That's the only way you can stay above the competition.

Knowledge is a commodity, as are apples or computers. Keep in mind that you can get it in many different ways. You don't need to know everything, but you need to be able to find someone to know for you. You need to be able to convince that person to share or help you assimilate your knowledge.

This is the main task of the entrepreneur. He is more of a talent coach than a visionary. It's not the skills of a single person that counts, but the whole group of people focused on a single project. As the author of this project, you may not have the slightest idea about it, but your leadership, negotiating and communication skills can help you acquire the knowledge you need without going to textbooks.

Knowledge is power only when it is used.

Ending

We have already finished our marathon. There are people waiting for her to admire our feat. Some give us water, others want to exchange a few words with us. Still barely breathing, we need to digest what we have just achieved. Success waited just behind the line of the forty-second kilometer.

We are tired and completely exhausted, but we are able to appreciate in the depths of consciousness what we have achieved. A person in love with long-distance running does not need a finish line or the admiration of the fans. It is enough for her to exceed a certain distance, which she intended to achieve in the allotted time.

Running and succeeding have a lot in common. Both of these activities teach humility and understanding for their own limitations. Thanks to them, you can also discover your strongest advantages, build a strong will and create your own image according to who you really wanted to be. The real run starts only when we lose the strength and motivation to take the next step, but it is at this point that the line between success and failure is set.

I trust that by following my advice, you will make better use of your own abilities. You have unlimited potential and it's up to you whether you cross the finish line or lag far behind other race participants.

Reading this book, you decided to stand up to the run, and although it is a success in itself, you can not let it get stuck somewhere in the middle of the route. Run at your own pace, but try to reach the finish line. Use everything to help you and keep looking for better solutions. Run forward, even if you catch your breath while you're in the process.

Everyone is waiting for you to show up at the finish line.

www.ingramcontent.com/pod-product-compliance
Lightning Source LLC
LaVergne TN
LVHW010651200726
843507LV00011B/1817